SMOKIN' SMILEYS
Coloring Book

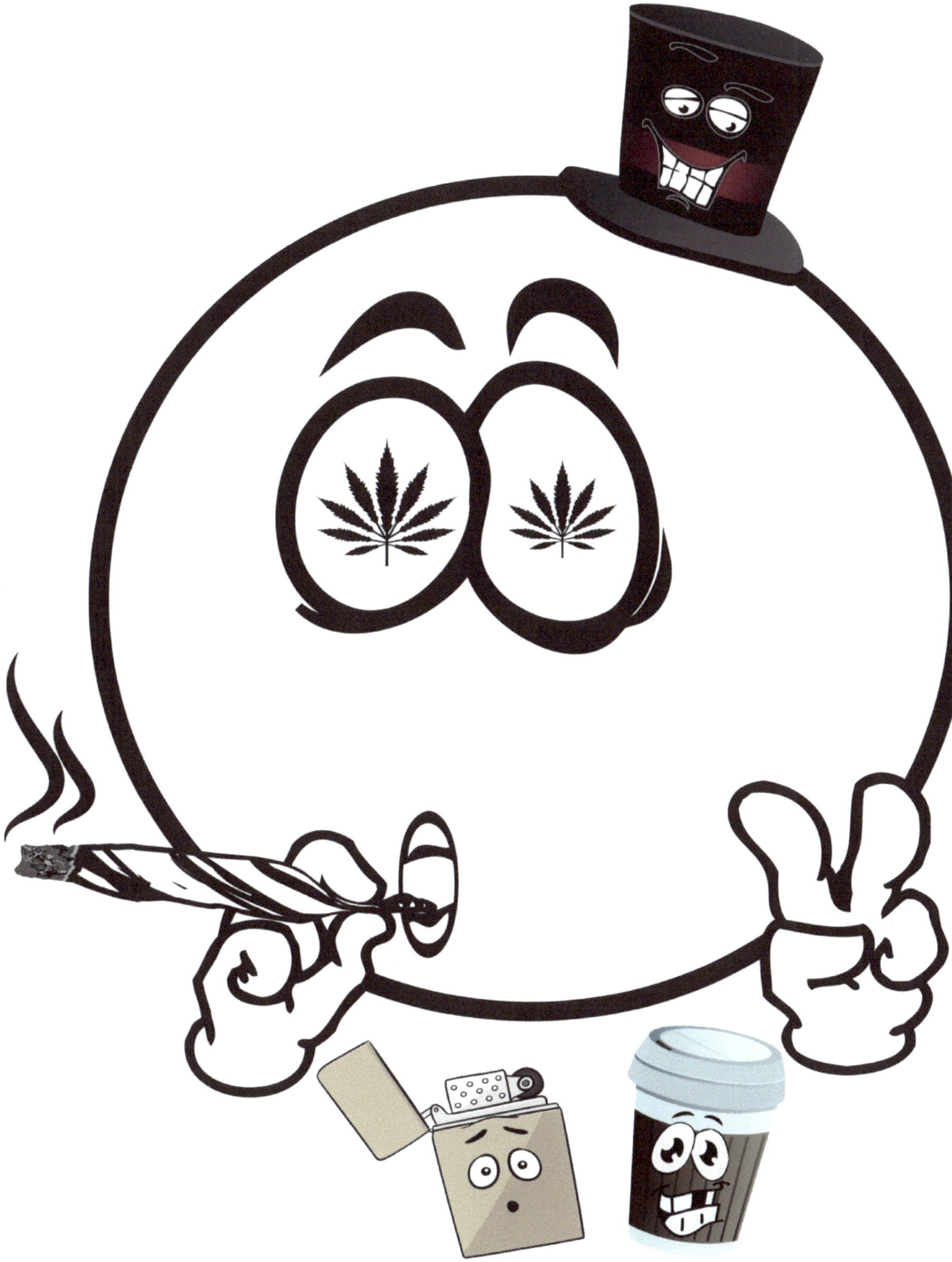

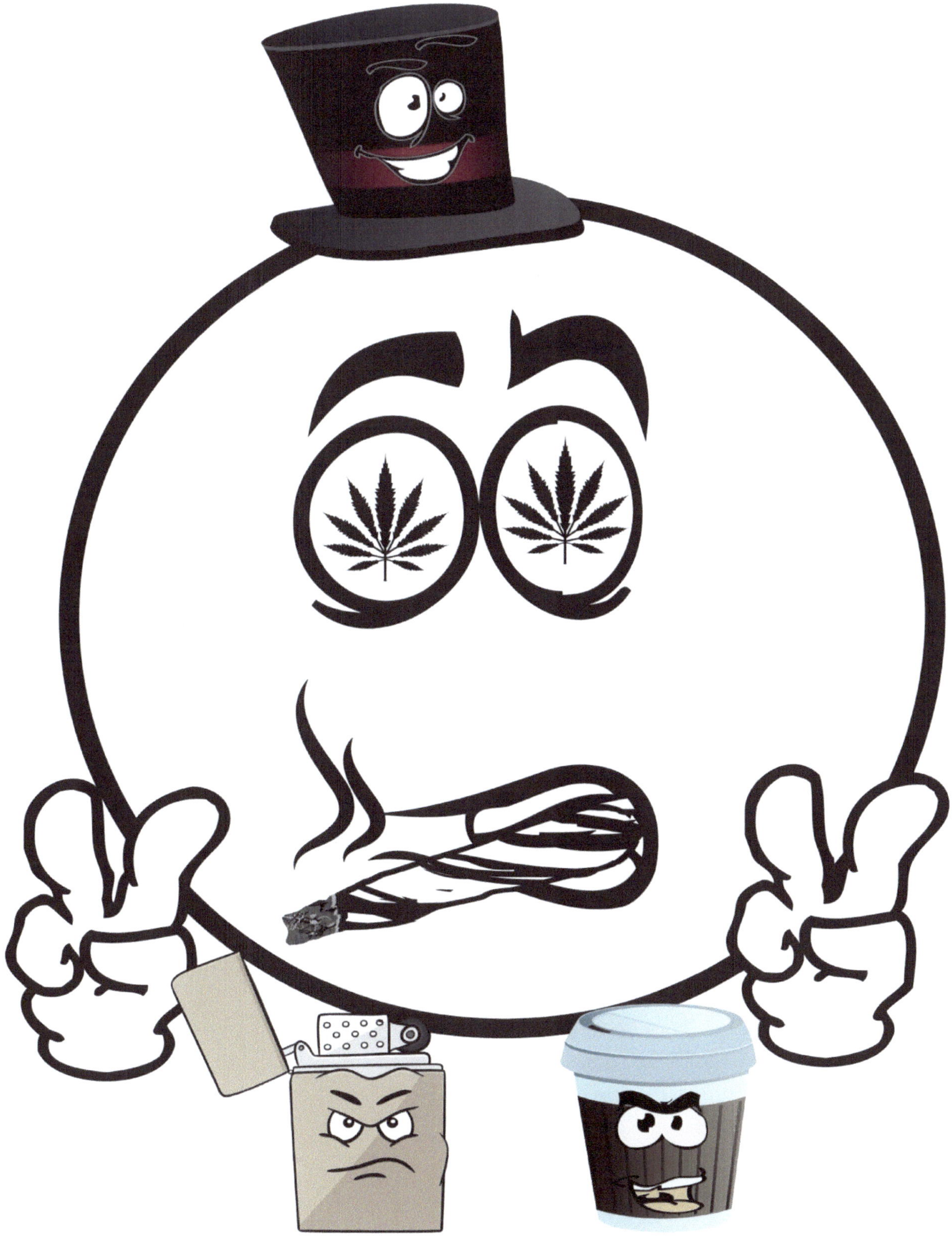

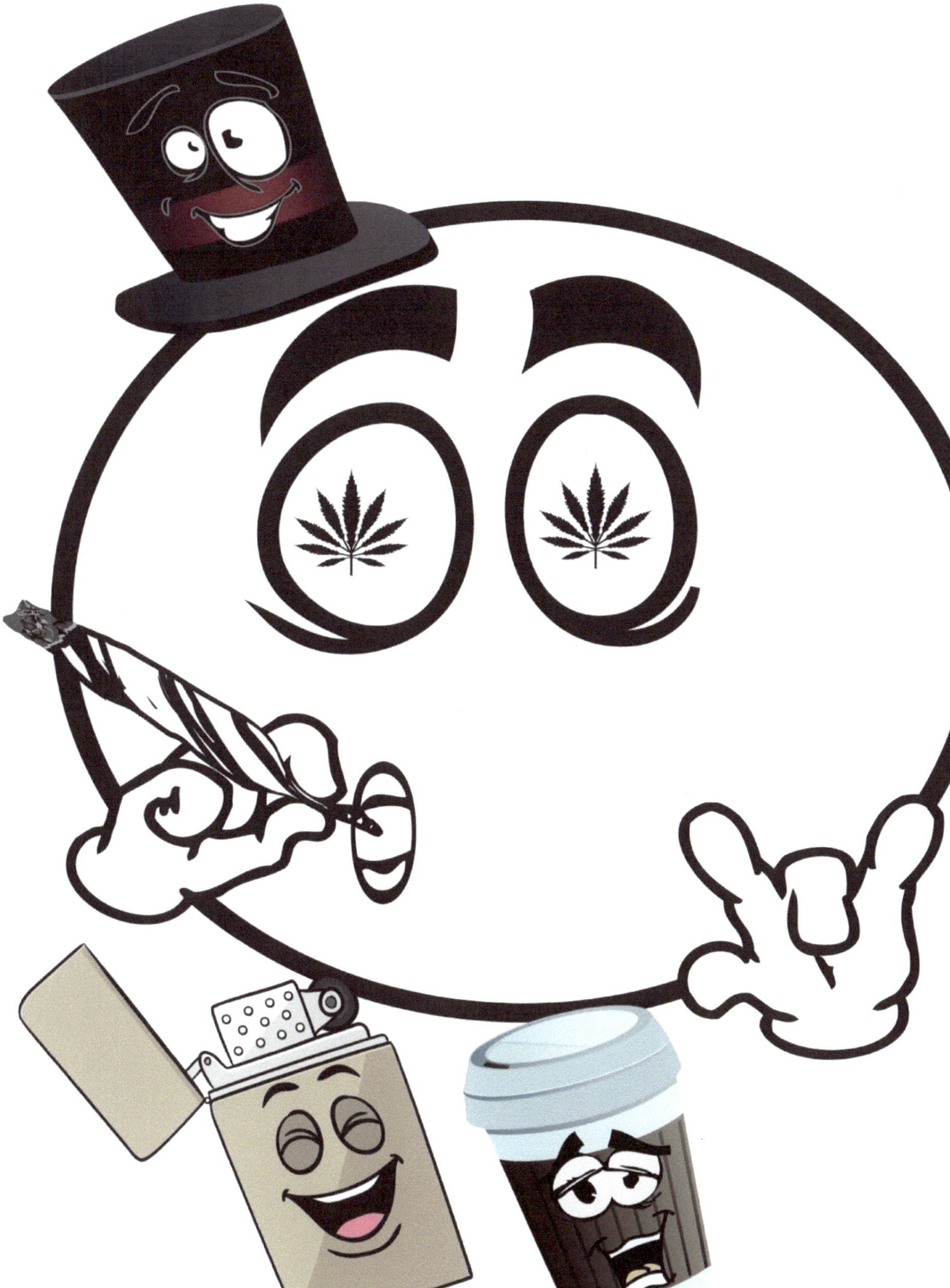

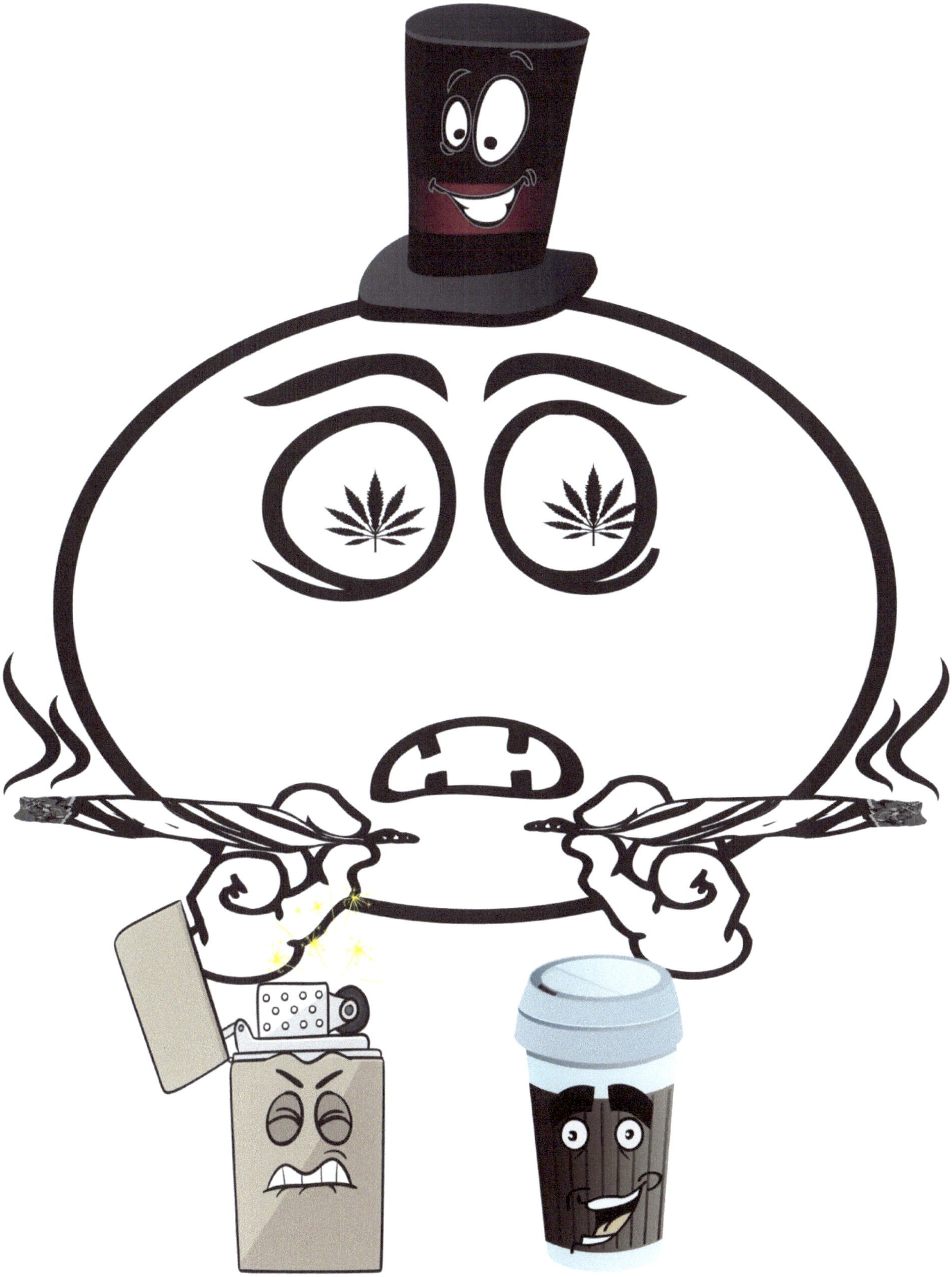

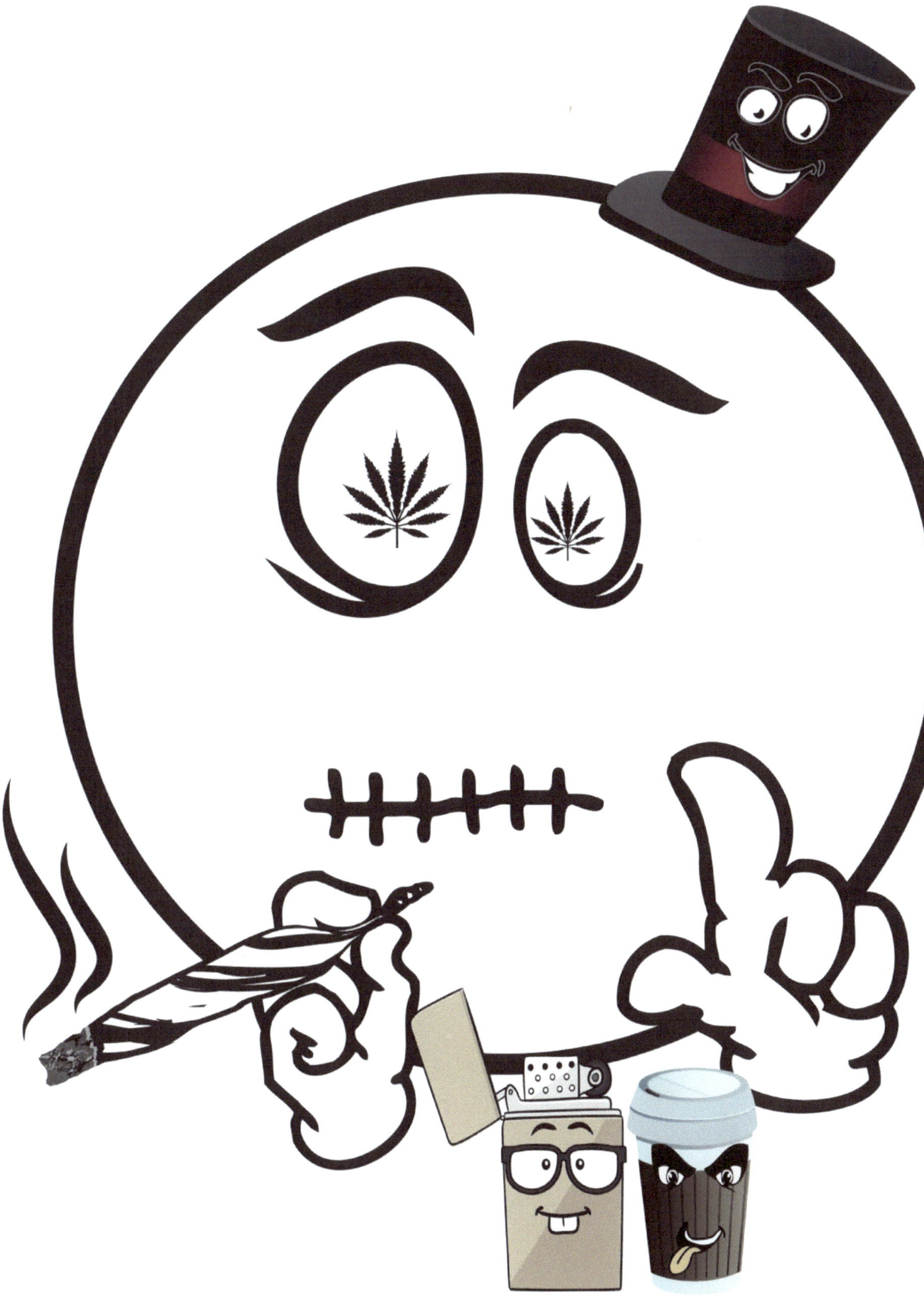

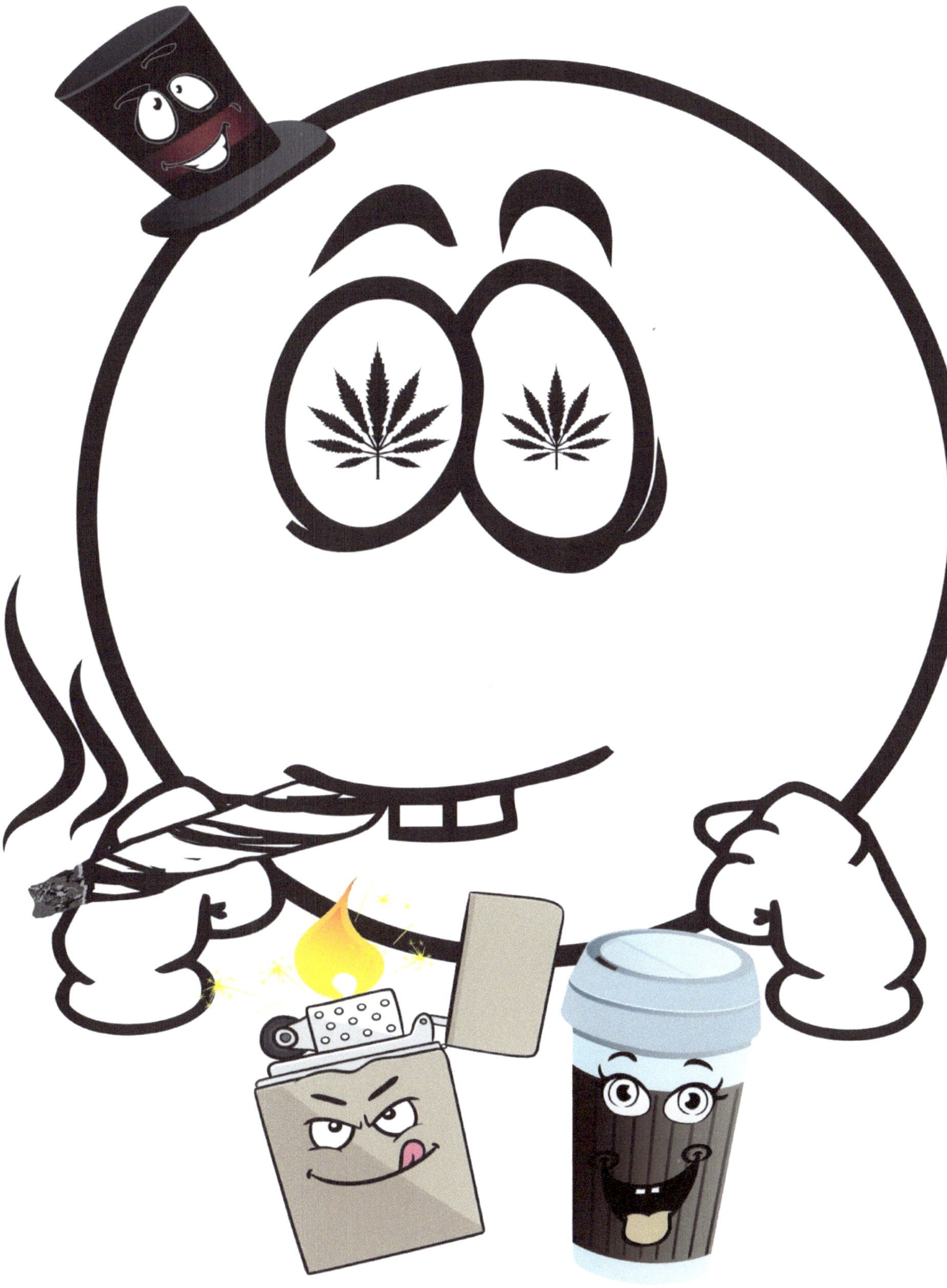

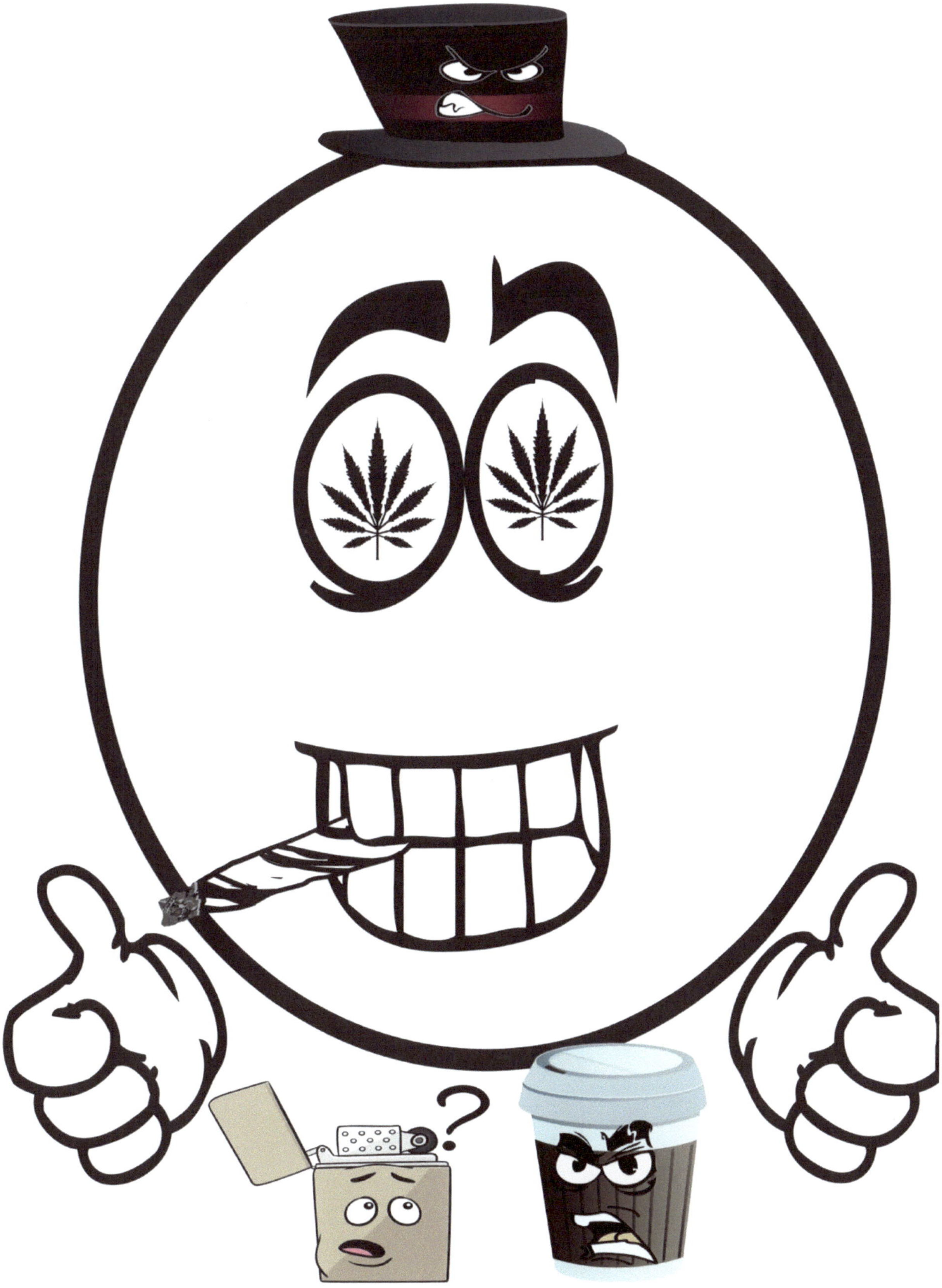

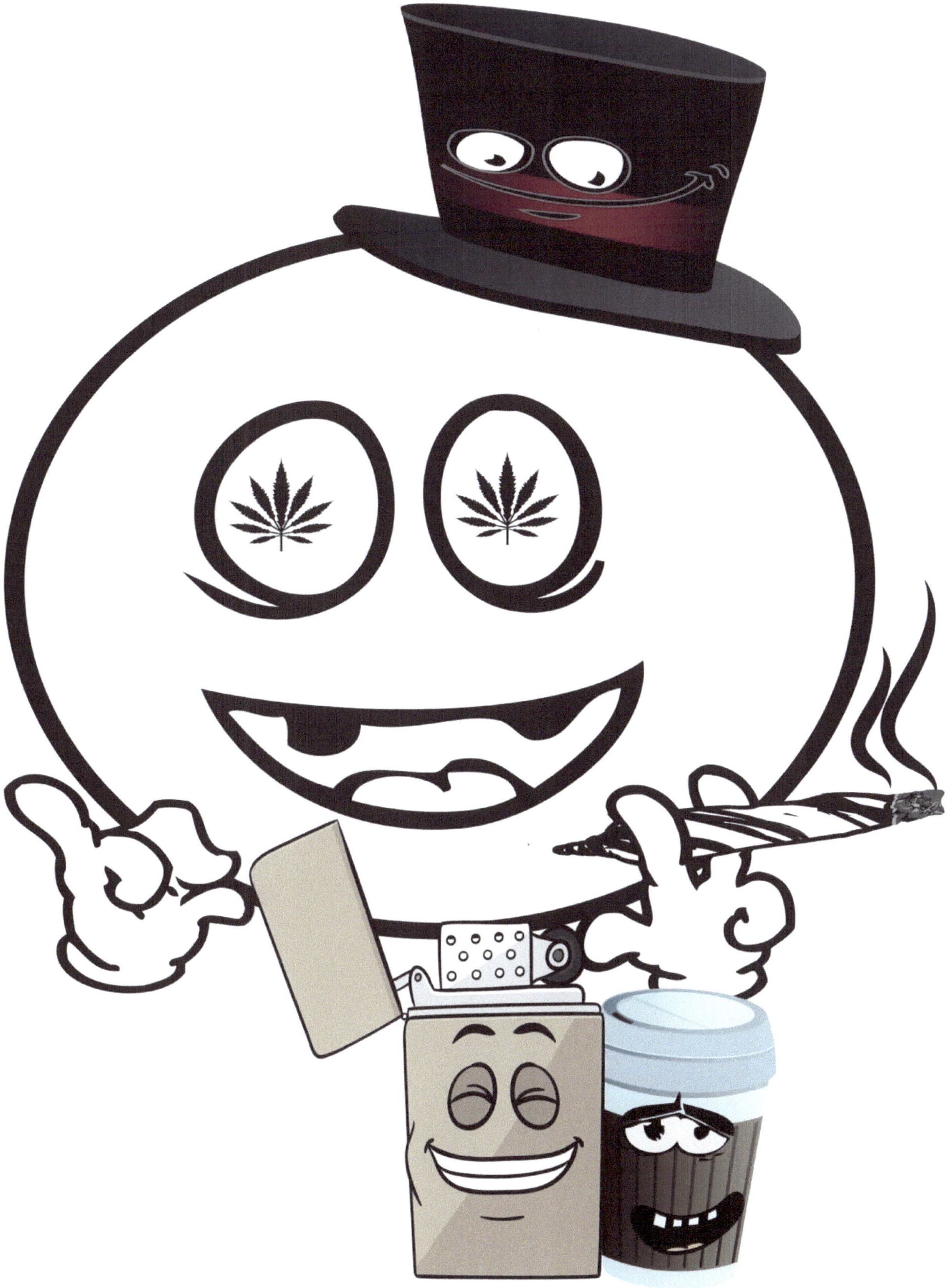

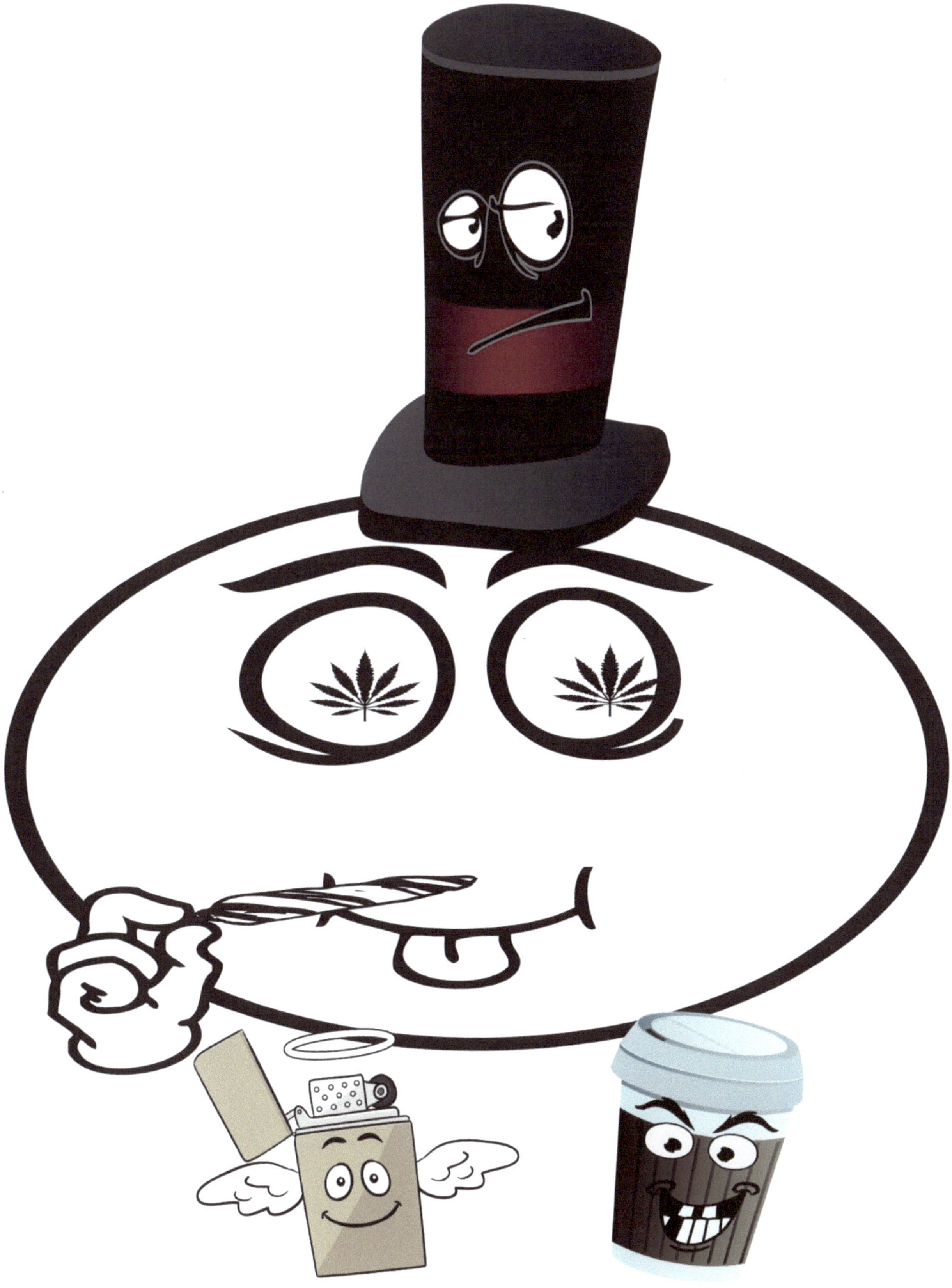

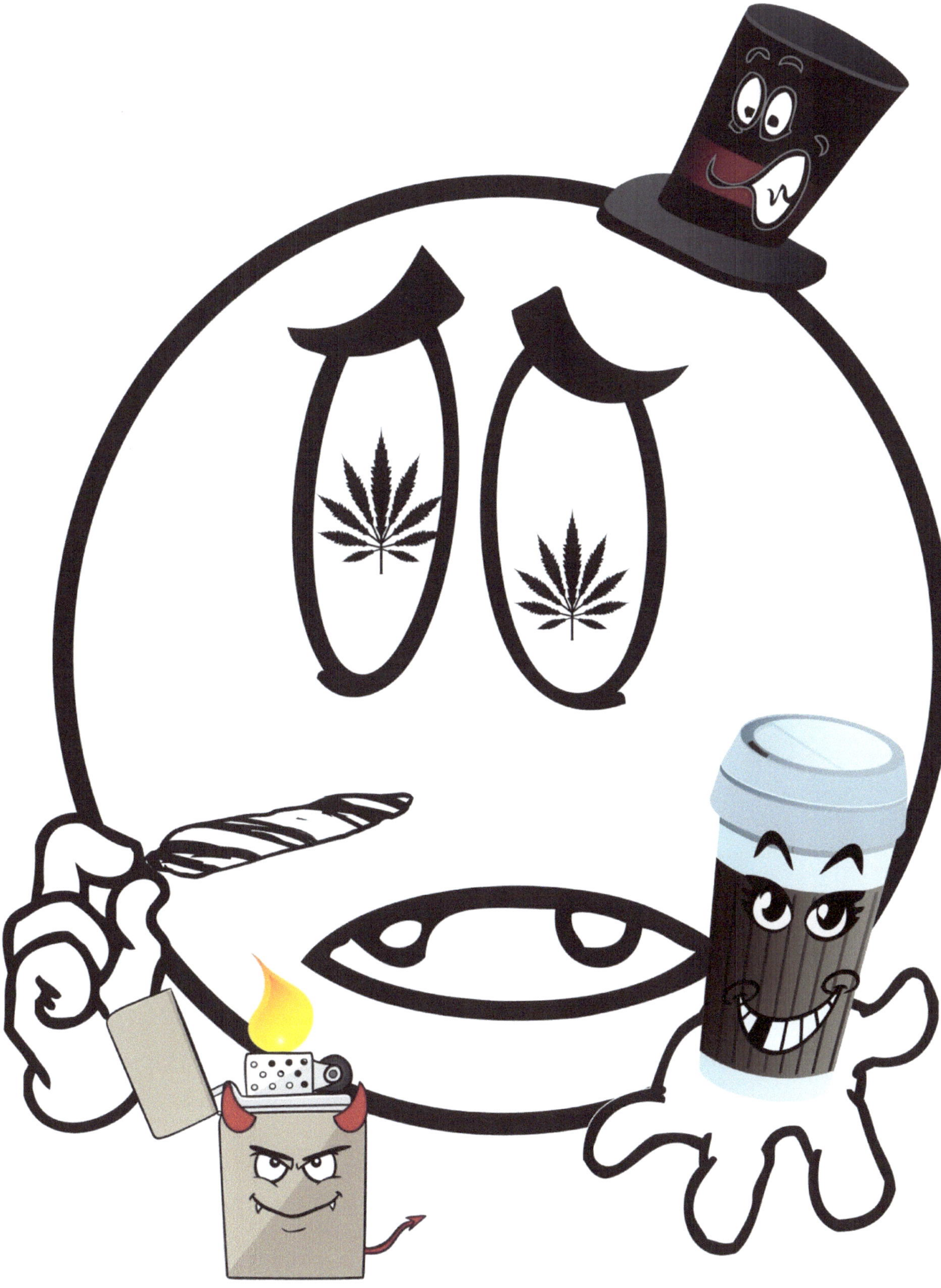

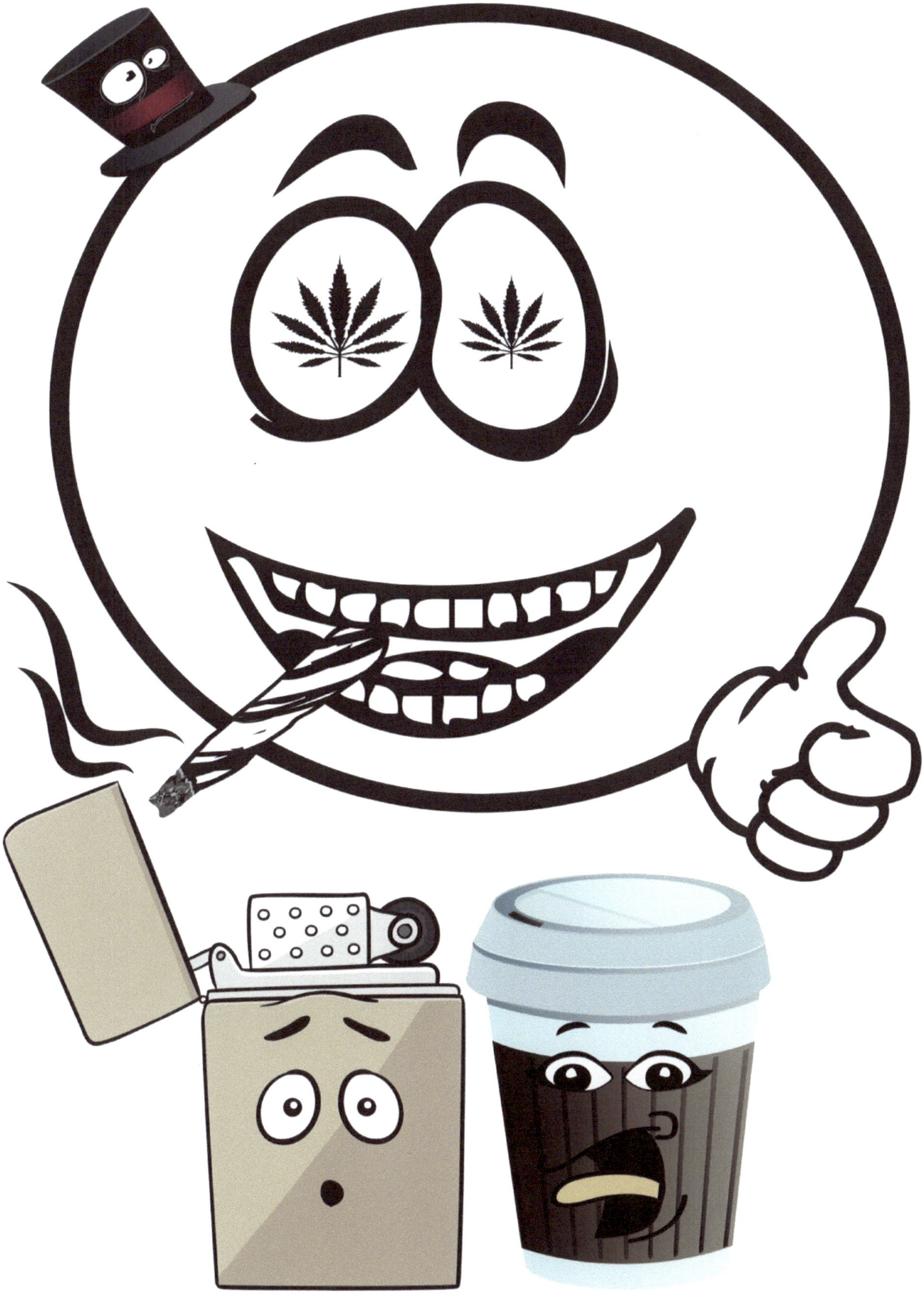

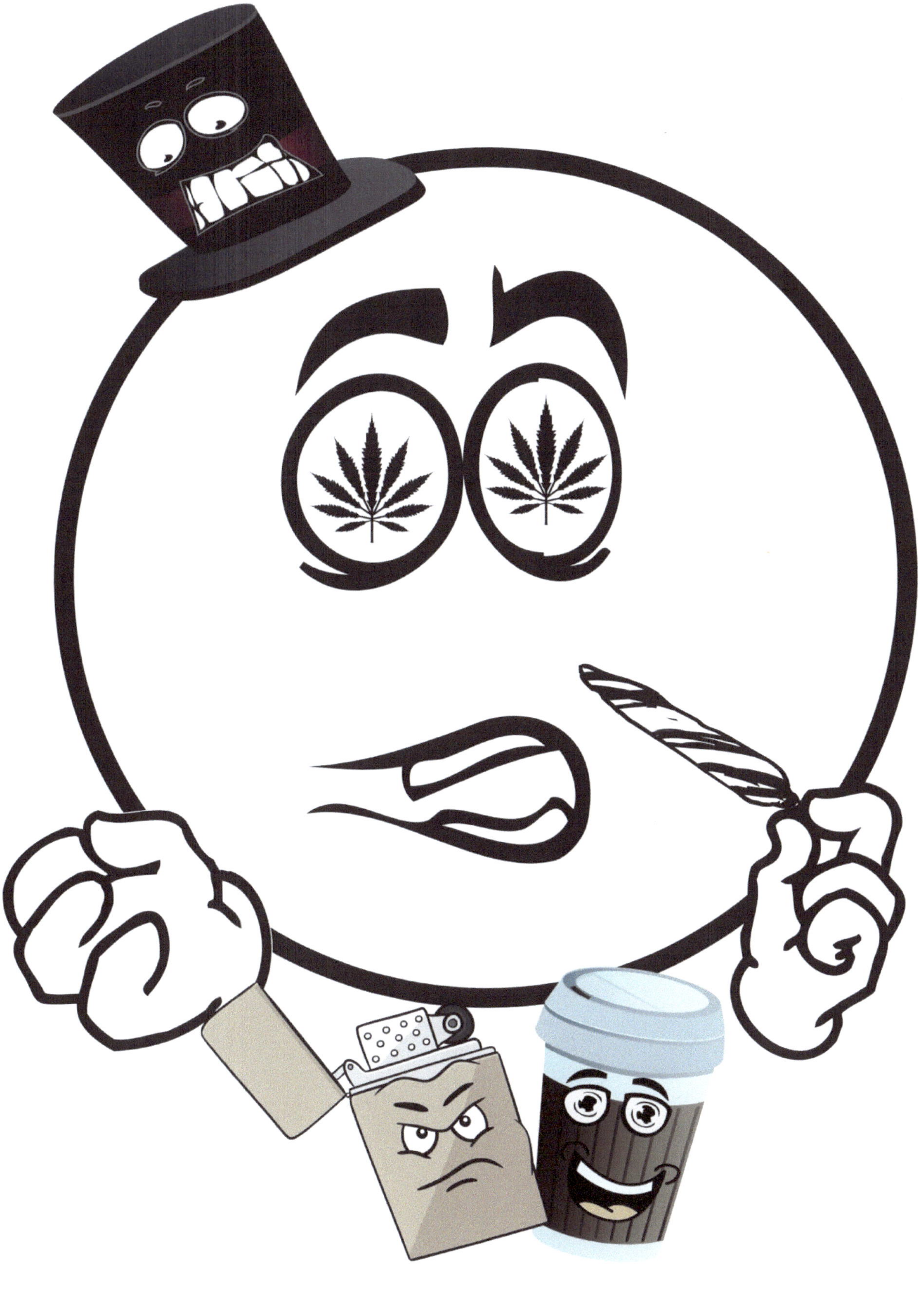

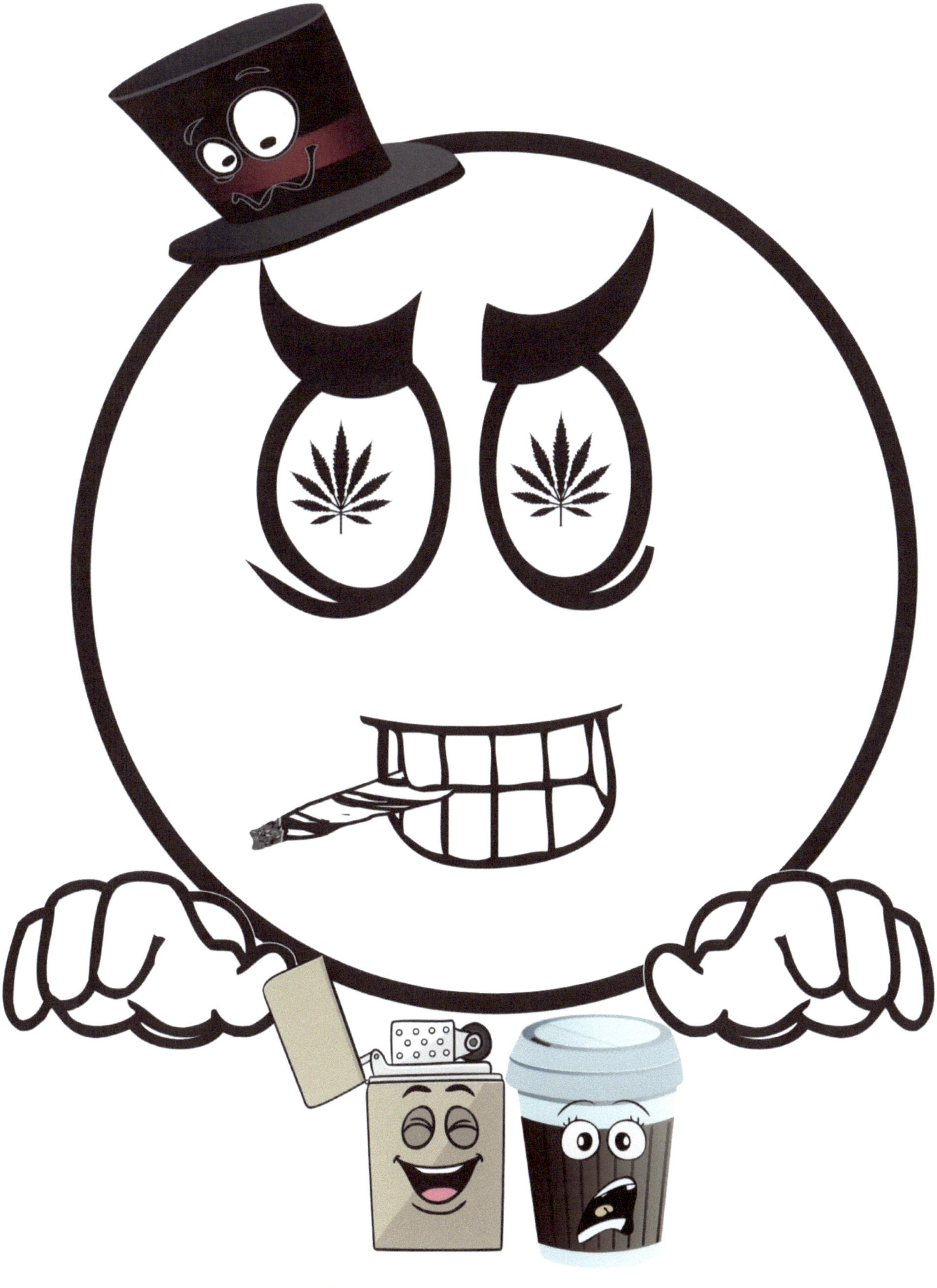

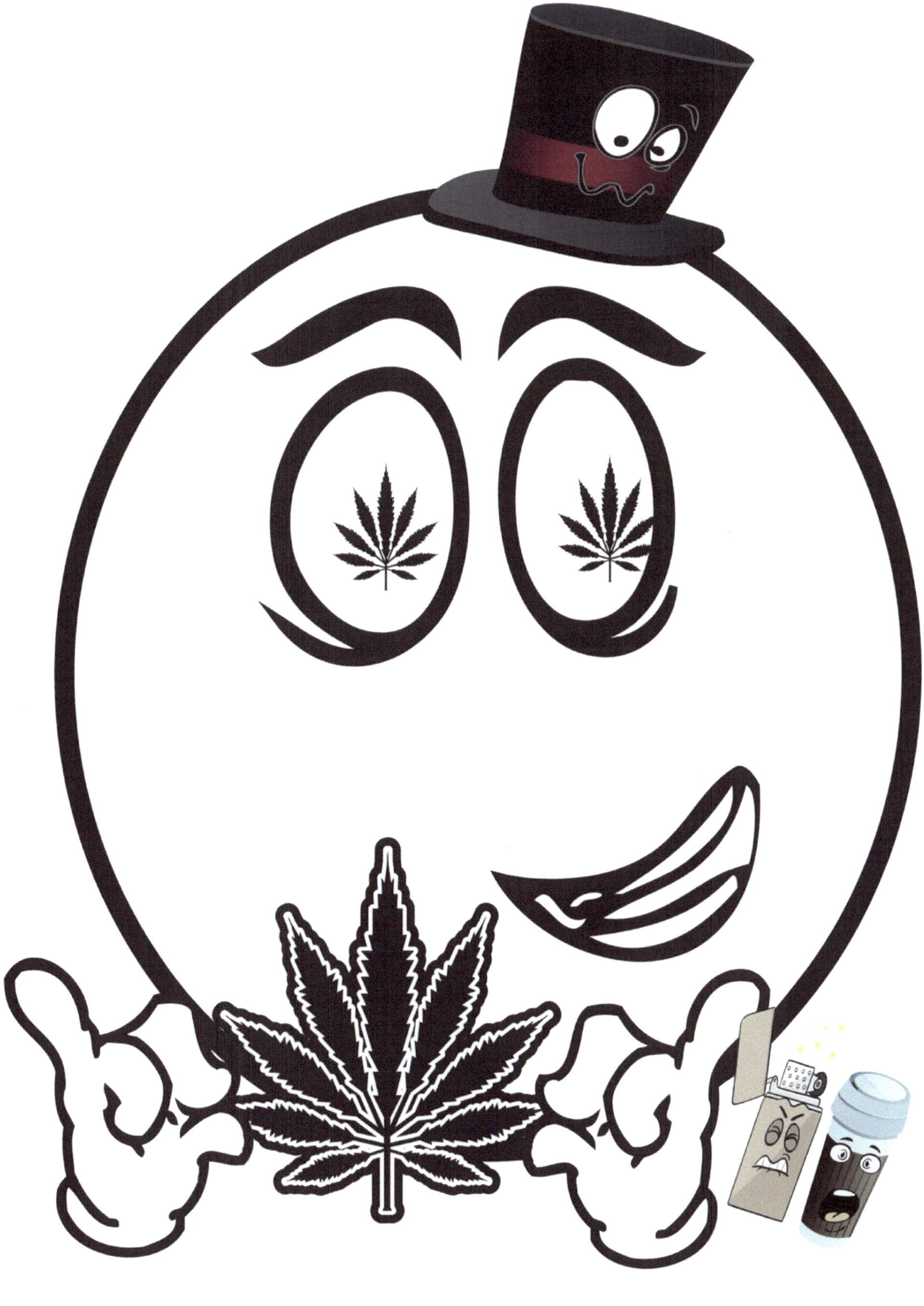

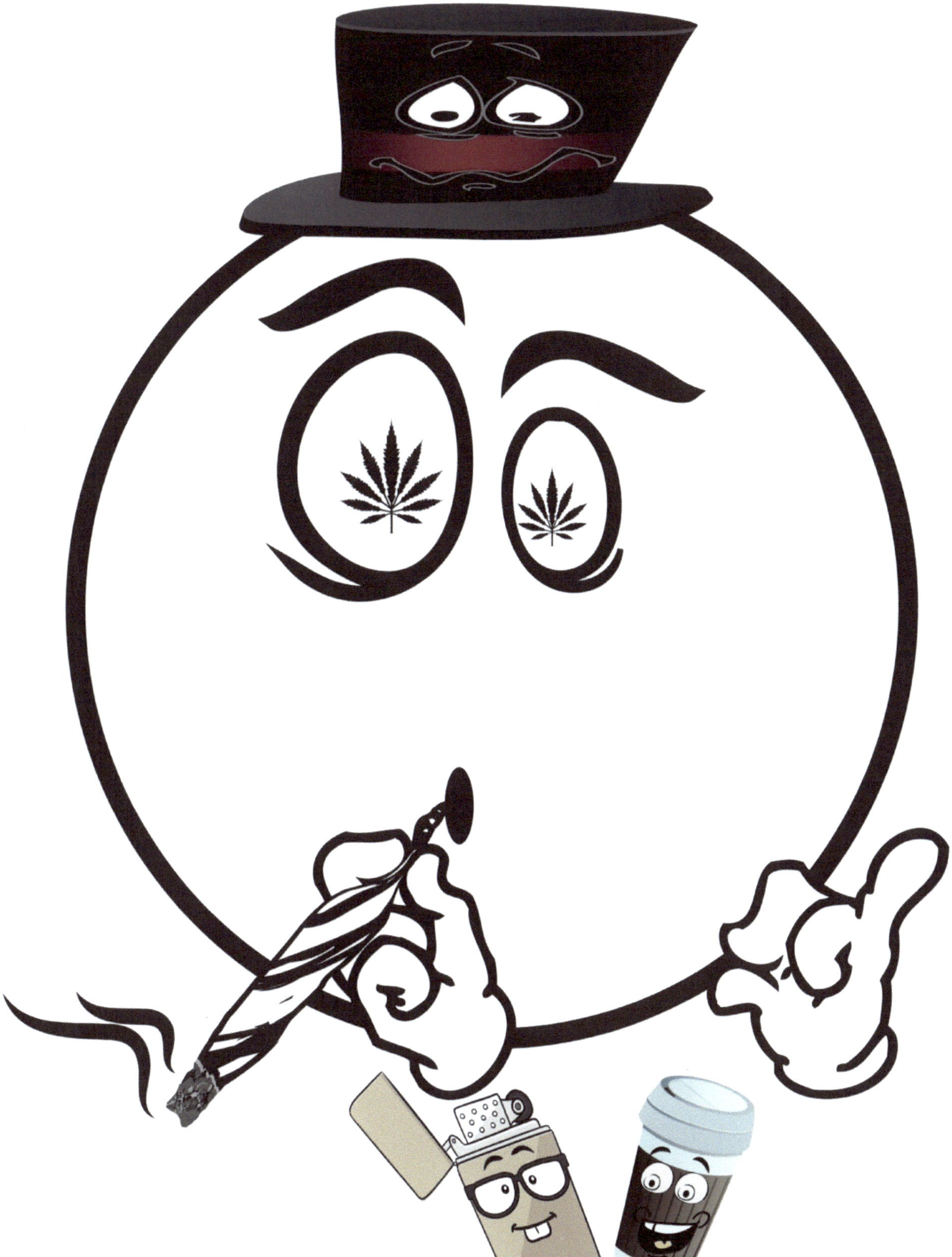

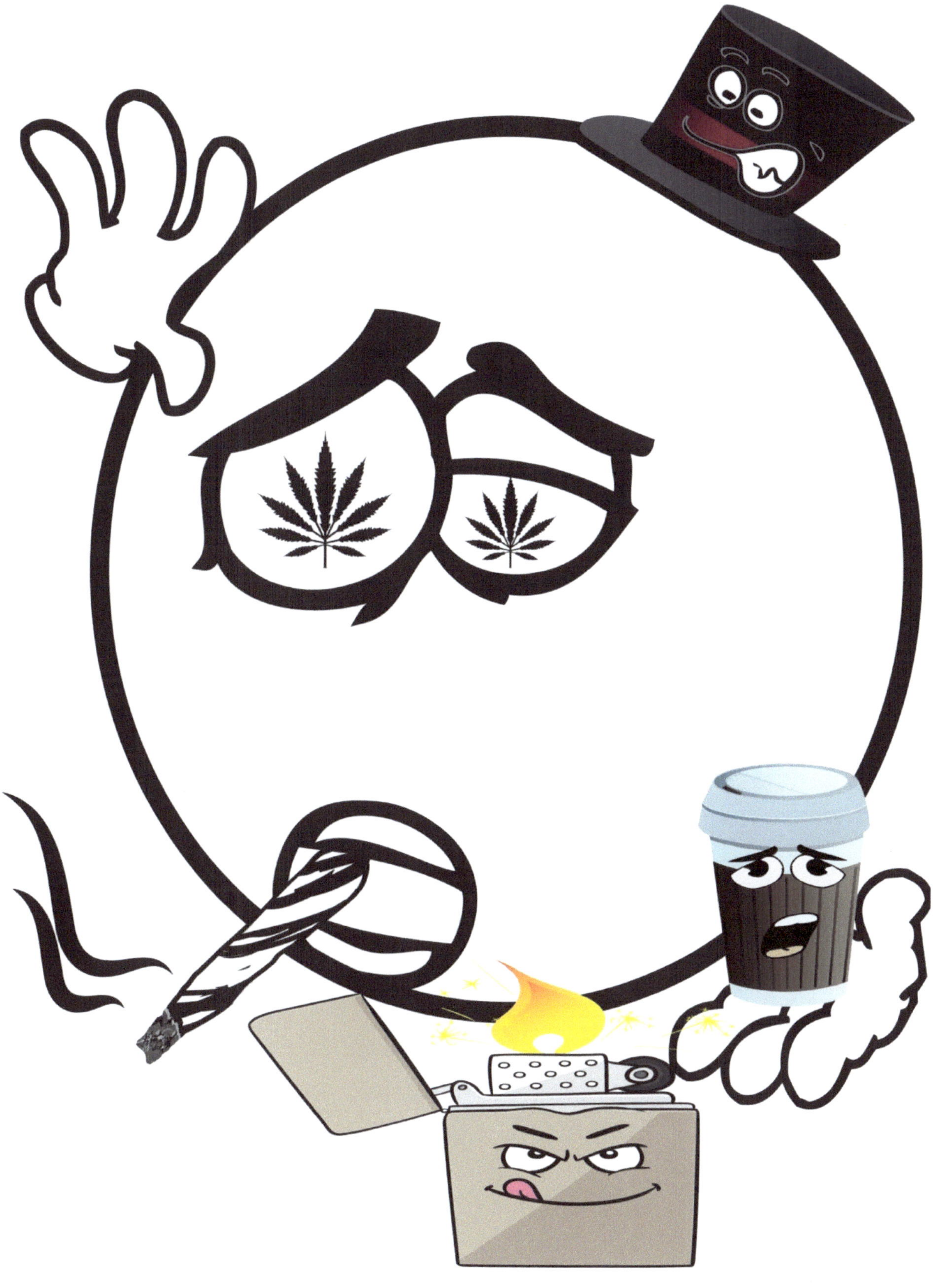

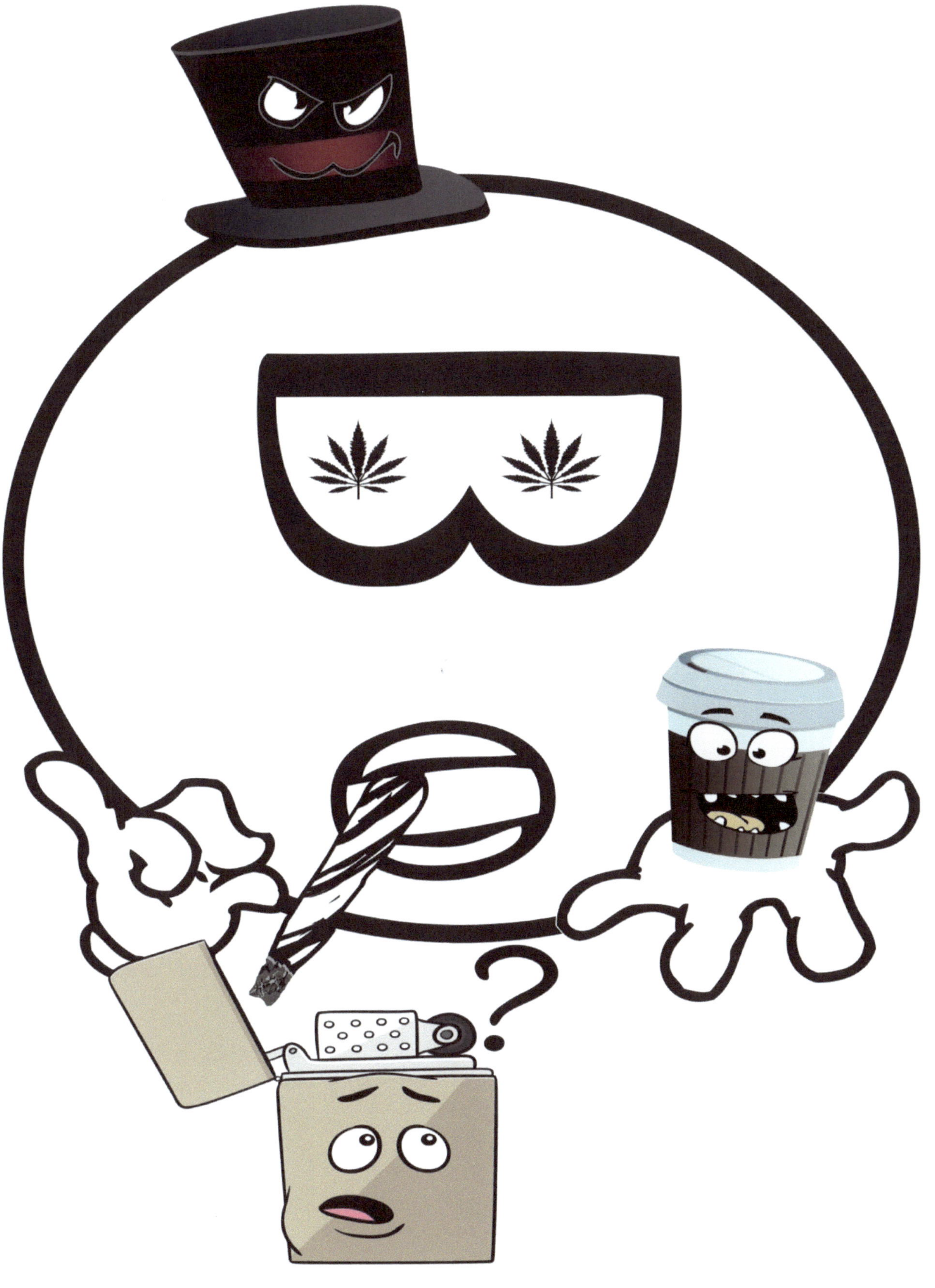

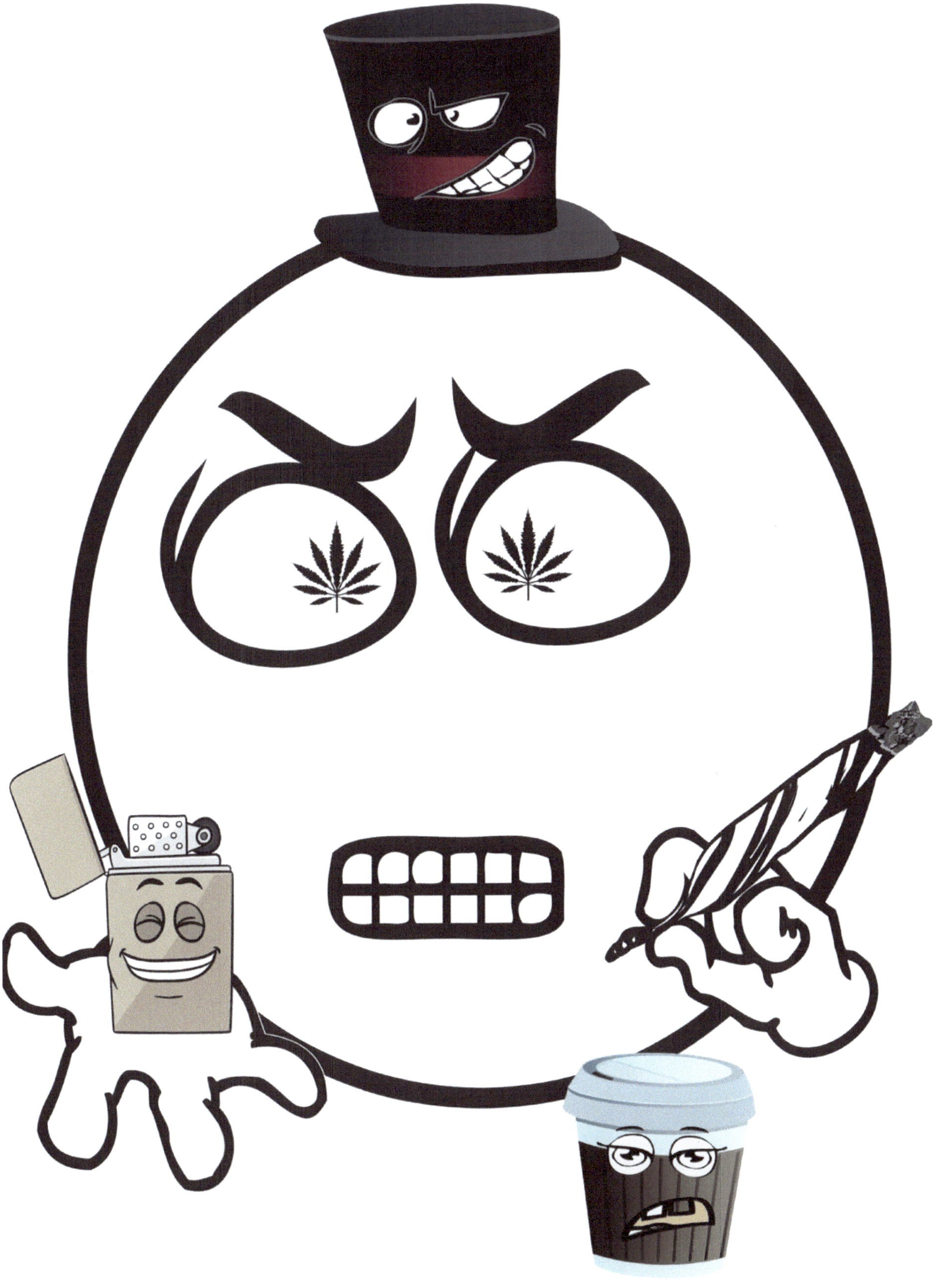

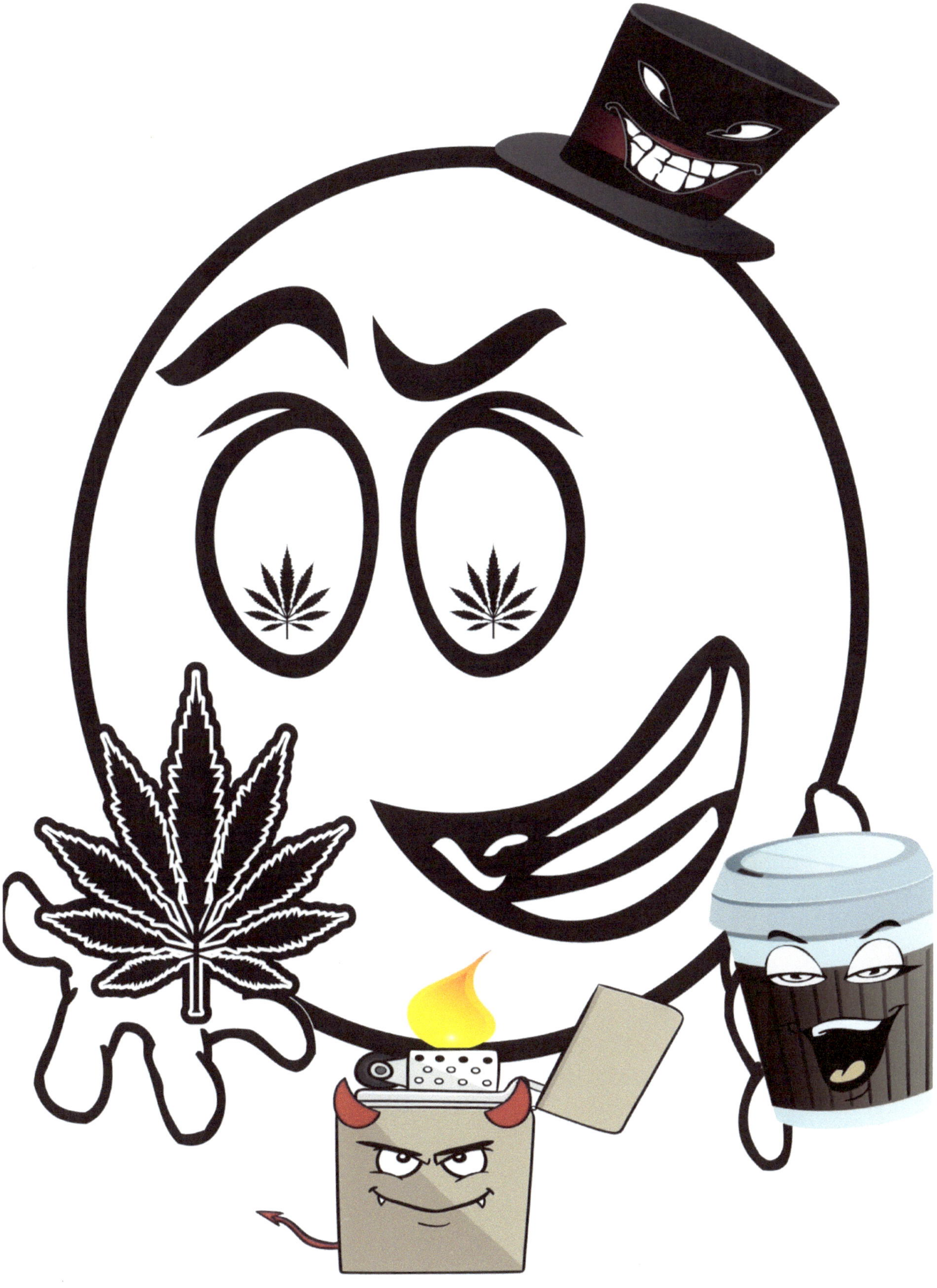

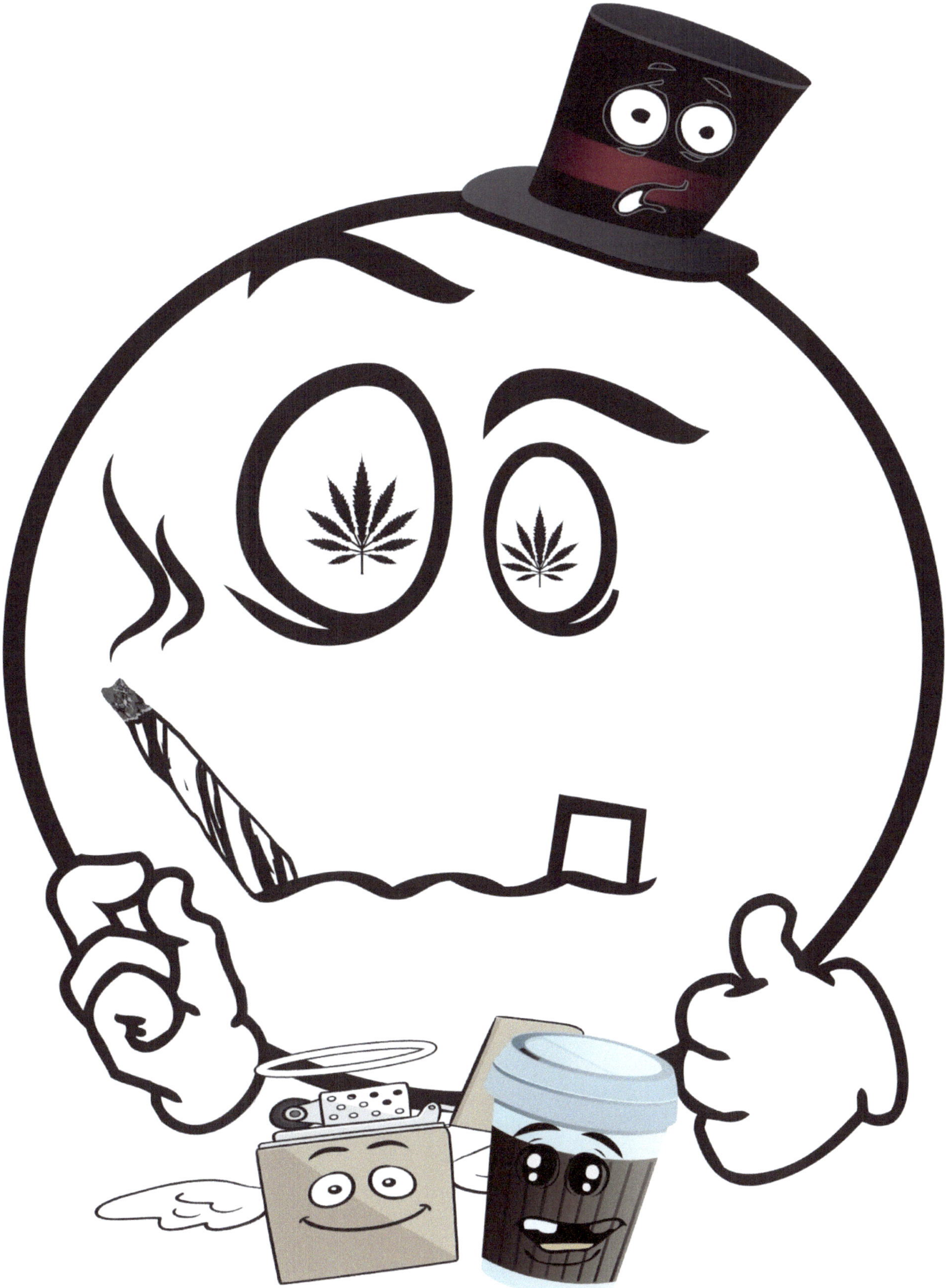

www.ingramcontent.com/pod-product-compliance
Lightning Source LLC
Chambersburg PA
CBHW050837180526
45159CB00004B/1938
* 9 7 8 1 5 1 7 5 0 0 8 5 6 *